STEP INTO HISTORY

SAIL!
Can You Command a Sea Voyage?

By Julia Bruce

Illustrated by Peter Dennis

Enslow Elementary

an imprint of

Enslow Publishers, Inc.
40 Industrial Road
Box 398
Berkeley Heights, NJ 07922
USA

http://www.enslow.com

Enslow Elementary, an imprint of Enslow Publishers, Inc.
Enslow Elementary® is a registered trademark of Enslow Publishers, Inc.

US edition published in 2009 by Enslow Publishers, Inc.
First published in 2007 by Orpheus Books Ltd.,
6 Church Green, Witney, Oxfordshire, OX28 4AW, England

Created and produced by
Julia Bruce, Rachel Coombs, Nicholas Harris, Sarah Hartley, and Erica Simms, Orpheus Books Ltd.
Text Julia Bruce
Illustrated by Peter Dennis *(Linda Rogers Associates)*
Consultants Professor Filipe Castro, Nautical Archaeology Program, Texas A&M University, and Brian Lavery

Library of Congress Cataloging-in-Publication Data
Bruce, Julia.
    Sail! can you command a sea voyage? / Julia Bruce.
        p. cm. — (Step into history)
    Includes bibliographical references and index.
    Summary: "Learn how to successfully complete a voyage from Portugal to India for spices in the 1500s" — Provided by publisher.
    ISBN-13: 978-0-7660-3477-8
    ISBN-10: 0-7660-3477-1
    1. Seafaring life—Juvenile literature. 2. Sailing ships—Juvenile literature. 3. Spice trade—History—Juvenile literature.
    I. Title
G540.B75 2009
910.4'5—dc22
                                                    2008019764

To Our Readers: We have done our best to make sure all Internet Addresses in this book were active and appropriate when we went to press. However, the author and the publisher have no control over and assume no liability for the material available on those Internet sites or on other Web sites they may link to. Any comments or suggestions can be sent by e-mail to comments@enslow.com or to the address on the back cover.

Printed and bound in China.

10 9 8 7 6 5 4 3 2 1

Contents

The Challenge

The year is 1593. The King of Portugal is planning to send a fleet of cargo ships to Portugal's colonies in India. He wants you, a brave and skilled captain, to command the fleet. It will sail from Portugal's capital, Lisbon, around the Cape of Good Hope at the southern tip of Africa. When you arrive at the Indian port of Goa, the ships will load up with pepper and luxury goods, such as silks and spices. You will then bring them back to Europe. The goods will then be sold for a huge profit. It is a great honor to be asked, but the voyage is long and dangerous.

It is possible to go to Goa and other parts of Asia over land routes. But those were closed off by local rulers in the middle of the fifteenth century. Besides, the king prefers to send his fleet traveling on sea routes. It's much faster and easier to transport goods in a large ship. There are fewer frontiers and borders to cross. It's also easier to defend against sea pirates than robbers on land.

Your ship is a huge vessel called a carrack or nau. It is designed to carry as much cargo as possible. You must make sure the ship has the crew, food, water, and other supplies needed to make the journey across thousands of miles and two oceans. Many dangers lie ahead. You and your crew must be ready for anything.

What supplies will you need to last you throughout the voyage? How will the crew navigate the ship and keep it on course? What can the crew and passengers do to stay healthy and strong along the way? Can the ship survive storms and possible attacks by pirates? Find out the answers to these questions and much more as you go through this sea voyage step-by-step. Can you successfully captain the ship on this exciting but dangerous voyage?

Route to India

The route to India from Europe is long and dangerous. You need to cross the open ocean and make your way through the stormy seas around the tip of Africa. To be successful, you must time your journey to avoid bad weather. You will use the ocean currents and winds to help you on your way. Try to follow the quickest and safest route.

 Beware of pirates! They are a real danger to your ships. There are also privateers. These are usually Dutch or English ships that have orders from their governments to attack ships from other countries and take their precious cargo.

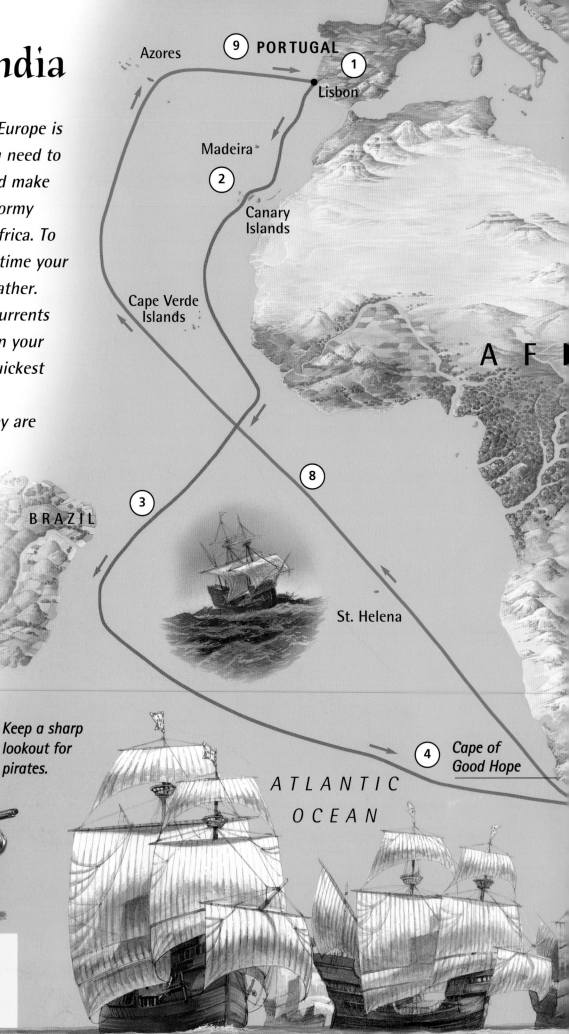

Azores

⑨ **PORTUGAL**

①

Lisbon

Madeira

②

Canary Islands

Cape Verde Islands

A F I

B R A Z I L

③

⑧

St. Helena

④ Cape of Good Hope

A T L A N T I C

O C E A N

Keep a sharp lookout for pirates.

KEY

→ *Outbound journey*

← *Return journey*

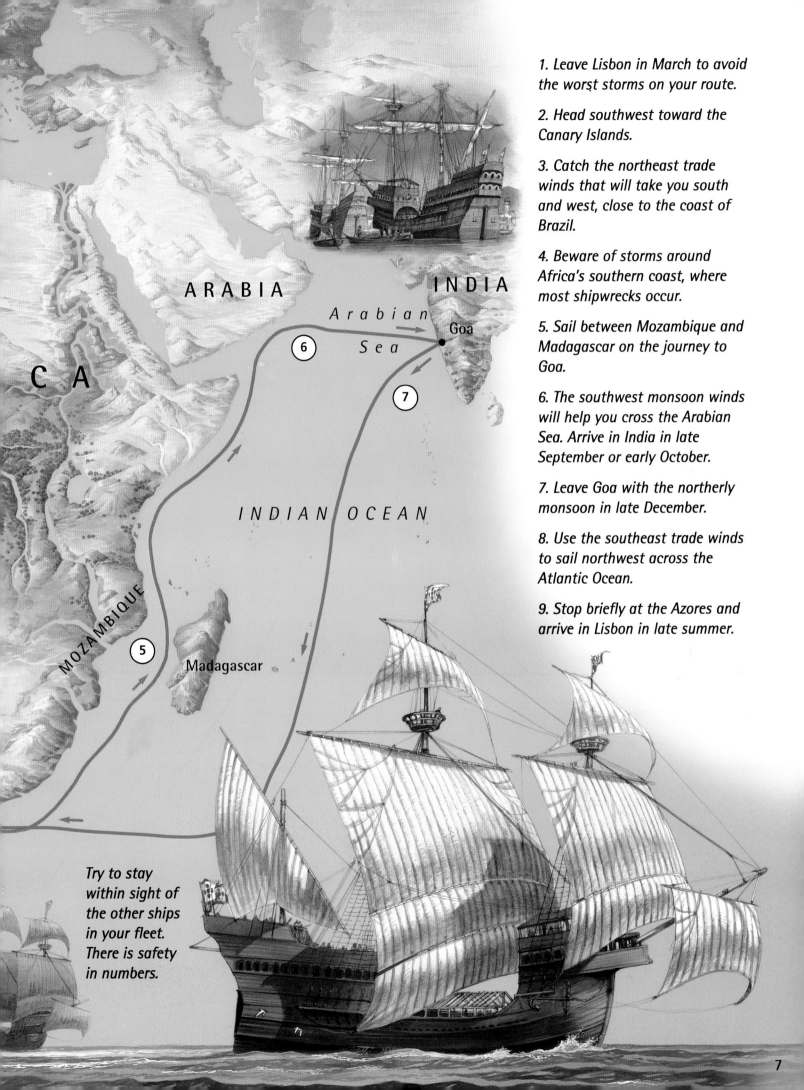

1. *Leave Lisbon in March to avoid the worst storms on your route.*

2. *Head southwest toward the Canary Islands.*

3. *Catch the northeast trade winds that will take you south and west, close to the coast of Brazil.*

4. *Beware of storms around Africa's southern coast, where most shipwrecks occur.*

5. *Sail between Mozambique and Madagascar on the journey to Goa.*

6. *The southwest monsoon winds will help you cross the Arabian Sea. Arrive in India in late September or early October.*

7. *Leave Goa with the northerly monsoon in late December.*

8. *Use the southeast trade winds to sail northwest across the Atlantic Ocean.*

9. *Stop briefly at the Azores and arrive in Lisbon in late summer.*

ARABIA

INDIA

Arabian

Goa

Sea

C A

INDIAN OCEAN

MOZAMBIQUE

Madagascar

Try to stay within sight of the other ships in your fleet. There is safety in numbers.

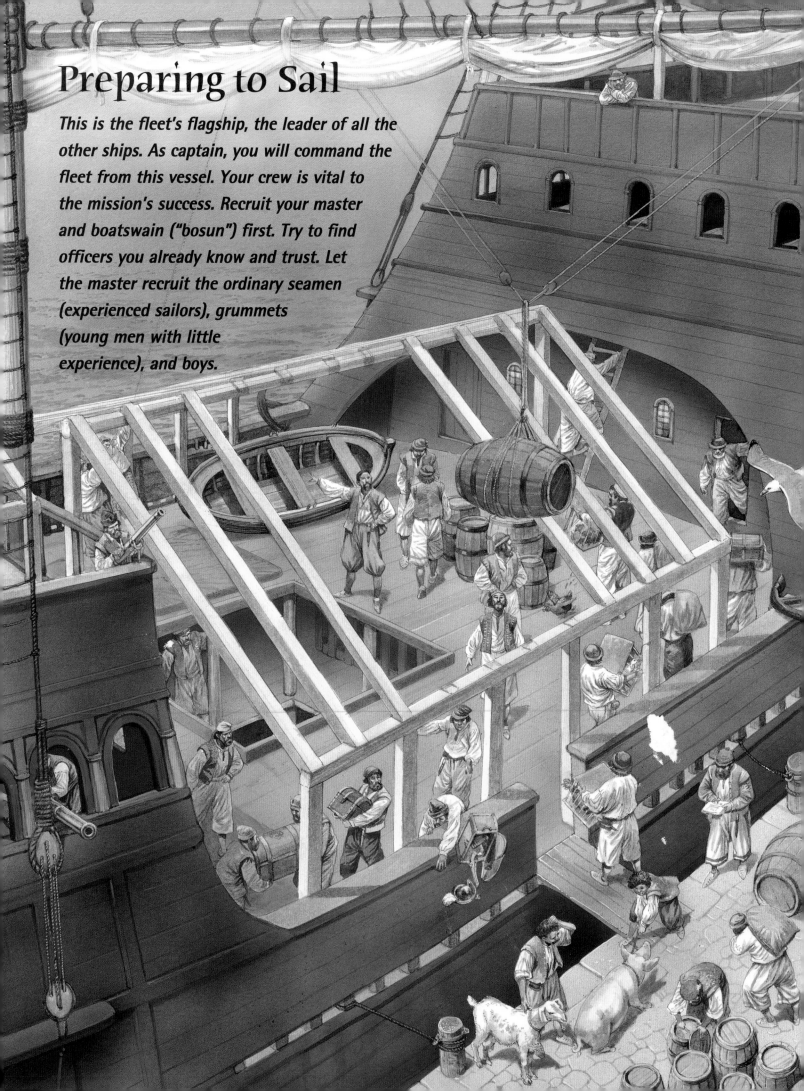

Preparing to Sail

This is the fleet's flagship, the leader of all the other ships. As captain, you will command the fleet from this vessel. Your crew is vital to the mission's success. Recruit your master and boatswain ("bosun") first. Try to find officers you already know and trust. Let the master recruit the ordinary seamen (experienced sailors), grummets (young men with little experience), and boys.

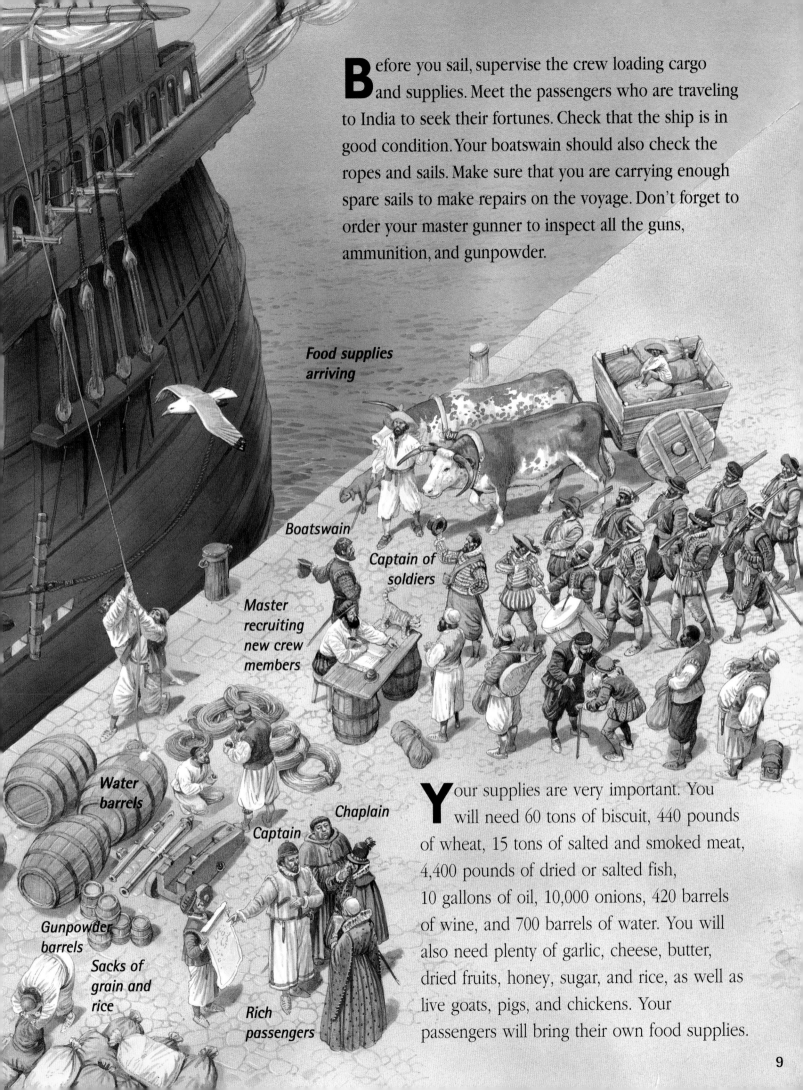

Before you sail, supervise the crew loading cargo and supplies. Meet the passengers who are traveling to India to seek their fortunes. Check that the ship is in good condition. Your boatswain should also check the ropes and sails. Make sure that you are carrying enough spare sails to make repairs on the voyage. Don't forget to order your master gunner to inspect all the guns, ammunition, and gunpowder.

Food supplies arriving

Boatswain

Captain of soldiers

Master recruiting new crew members

Chaplain

Captain

Water barrels

Gunpowder barrels

Sacks of grain and rice

Rich passengers

Your supplies are very important. You will need 60 tons of biscuit, 440 pounds of wheat, 15 tons of salted and smoked meat, 4,400 pounds of dried or salted fish, 10 gallons of oil, 10,000 onions, 420 barrels of wine, and 700 barrels of water. You will also need plenty of garlic, cheese, butter, dried fruits, honey, sugar, and rice, as well as live goats, pigs, and chickens. Your passengers will bring their own food supplies.

Passengers and Crew

Master Grummet Boatswain

Pilot

You will have at least 400 people on board: soldiers, passengers, the crew, and servants. There are many officers under your command to help you keep order. The master is your second-in-command. He supervises the crew. He's also in charge of the day-to-day running of the ship. The captain of the soldiers is in charge of his 250 men-at-arms. You are in charge of everyone, including all passengers and crew.

Chaplain and boys singing | Teaching knot tying | Captain and clerk

The pilot is in charge of navigation. Either the pilot or the underpilot is on deck at all times making sure the ship is on course. The boatswain checks the sails and rigging. He also supervises the men working at either end of the ship, which is called the stern at the back and bow at the front.

Cross-section of the canopy support to show the deck.

Passengers

Skilled carpenters and coopers, or barrel-makers, are important members of your crew. The carpenter and his apprentices make repairs to the ship. The cooper checks that the barrels for storing food, wine, and water are in good condition and do not leak. If your cooper does not do his job well, you risk losing valuable food supplies. Rotting food and wine and water going bad can lead to hunger, sickness, and even death on board.

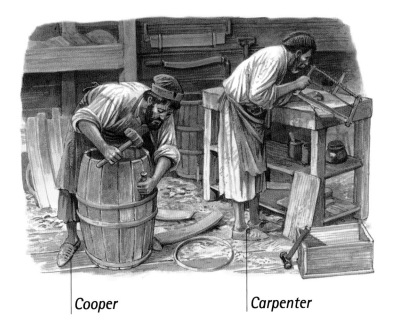

Cooper   *Carpenter*

Doctor

The ship must have a doctor who will keep an eye on your crew's general health. The doctor must also be able to perform surgery such as removing limbs, stitching wounds, or setting broken bones. Make sure your doctor has a good reputation and enough medicine and supplies.

Your clerk will help you keep track of events during the voyage and record food eaten and supplies used. The clerk also supervises the loading and unloading of cargo in India. Make sure he records any punishments you give out—and any deaths.

Captain

Clerk

The crew off-duty

Chickens

Ordinary seamen, grummets, and boys do many things on board. They man the sails, swab the decks, and pump the bilges. The chaplain takes care of them and teaches their lessons. He also conducts daily services for the entire ship. Your passengers include merchants, nobles, and priests. Some of the women on board include servants and passengers' wives.

AFTCASTLE

The captain of the soldiers should drill the men daily, and make sure they keep their guns clean and well oiled.

1 Log party
2 Rudder
3 Captain's quarters
4 Tiller
5 Officers' quarters
6 Gun cleaning
7 Doctor
8 Carpenter
9 Helm and whipstaff
10 Pepper boxes
11 Pilot and master
12 Passengers
13 Bilges
14 Soldiers
15 Food stores
16 Prisoner
17 Bilge pump
18 Main mast
19 Stove
20 Launch
21 Water barrels
22 Crew
23 Gunpowder store
24 Canopy support
25 Chapel
26 Grummets and boys
27 Crew and soldiers
28 Coopers
29 Grain stores
30 Foremast
31 Latrine
32 Spare sails
33 Spare ropes

Down in the hold, there are many boxes that will be used to store loose peppercorns, your main cargo from India. The rest of the hold is packed with other goods and food supplies. Every inch of spare space will be filled with spices, silks, and other luxury items on the return voyage from India.

Your ship is large, but it is also very crowded with so many people on board. You and your officers have your own cabins in the forecastle (pronounced FOK-sul) and aftcastle (AF-sul). These are the raised sections at the front and rear of the ship. Wealthy passengers also have their own rooms in the stern. Ordinary crew, soldiers, and servants must all find places for themselves and their belongings on the lower decks.

Know the Ship

Grummets and boys sleep on the weather deck under the forecastle.

FORECASTLE

Your crew should clean the ship daily and pump out the bilges, which soon fill up with filthy water.

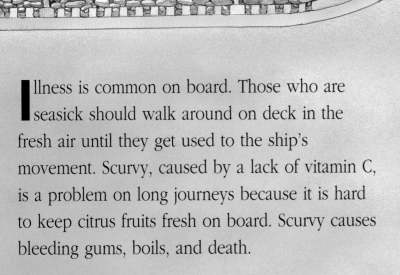

Illness is common on board. Those who are seasick should walk around on deck in the fresh air until they get used to the ship's movement. Scurvy, caused by a lack of vitamin C, is a problem on long journeys because it is hard to keep citrus fruits fresh on board. Scurvy causes bleeding gums, boils, and death.

Keeping everyone busy on the long voyage is a big challenge. An idle crew is more likely to cause trouble than a busy one. It is wise to keep them occupied even in their spare time. Make sure your chaplain holds services a few times a day. Encourage the crew to play music, dance, and entertain each other. Those with skills such as reading the weather and operating the guns should teach others, including interested passengers. Discourage gambling and card playing at all costs. These activities can lead to violent disputes.

Keeping the Vessel Shipshape

All upper decks must be scrubbed clean each Sunday morning before services. A block of sandstone will help scrape off the grime. The gaps between the planks must be sealed regularly to stop water from getting through. To do this, soak a rope in tar. Then use a caulking iron to push the rope into the cracks.

Using a sandstone

Caulking to seal joints between planks

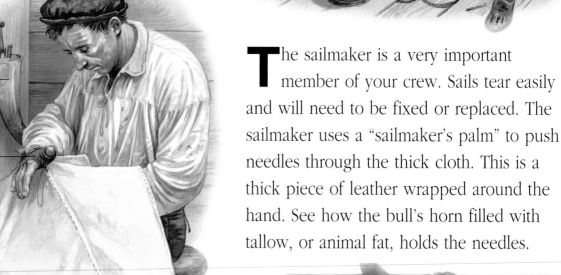

A bull's horn filled with tallow

Sailmaker's palm

The sailmaker is a very important member of your crew. Sails tear easily and will need to be fixed or replaced. The sailmaker uses a "sailmaker's palm" to push needles through the thick cloth. This is a thick piece of leather wrapped around the hand. See how the bull's horn filled with tallow, or animal fat, holds the needles.

Be sure to have the master gunner check and clean the guns often. A pirate attack could happen anytime, so it's best to be ready. Your master gunner should make sure that all members of the crew know how to prepare and fire the guns. Don't overlook the details, such as how to use a shot gauge to make sure the cannonballs will fit the muzzle.

Using shot gauge

Barrel of gunpowder

Boiling water pot | Soldiers' stove | General stove

Food bag

Sand box | Water | Crewmen and servants

ooking must be strictly organized. If you have two stoves, assign one to the soldiers and the other to passengers and crew. Give clear orders about who can use the stove and when. Passengers and officers (or at least their servants) should be first, then crewmen, grummets, and boys.

Officers dining

toves should be either tiled or metal boxes placed in sand to keep sparks from flying out and causing fires. Do not let anyone light the fires if the seas are rough. Buckets of water should always be nearby to put out any fires. The clerk should give out food supplies daily. Several bags of food can be cooked in boiling water at the same time. Tell passengers and crew to choose one or two people to cook for a group. That way there are not too many people trying to use the stove at once.

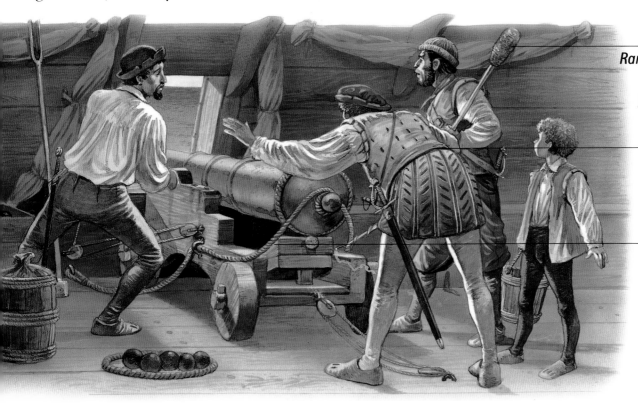

Rammer for pushing cannonballs and powder down the barrel

Master gunner

Rope to prevent the cannon from moving too much

Navigation

One of the greatest challenges of your voyage is finding your way across thousands of miles of ocean. You must depend on your pilot to keep you on course, so be sure to recruit the best. The pilot figures out the ship's position, speed, and direction. The pilot also gives orders to the boatswain and the helm, who steers the ship by adjusting the rudder and the sails. The pilot uses many different instruments and techniques to navigate.

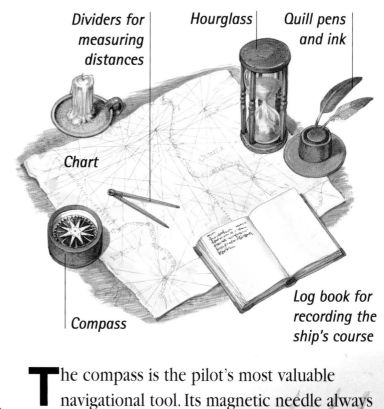

Dividers for measuring distances

Hourglass

Quill pens and ink

Chart

Log book for recording the ship's course

Compass

The compass is the pilot's most valuable navigational tool. Its magnetic needle always points north. Using a compass, the pilot knows which direction the ship is traveling in. Time is measured using hourglasses. Charts are also used for keeping track of the ship's position.

Using a cross-staff

Adjust the cross-piece until the top is in line with the sun, and the bottom with the horizon.

Swinging the lead

Latitude means how far north or south of the Equator the ship is. To figure this out, the pilot measures the height of the sun at noon using a cross-staff. This height changes as your latitude changes.

To find the ship's latitude at night, your pilot can use an astrolabe (pronounced AST-ro-LABE). The pilot measures the angle between the North Star, his eye, and the horizon. He turns the pointer on the astrolabe until it is lined up with the star. Then he reads the angle marked by the pointer on the outside rim of the instrument.

Finding out longitude—how far east or west you are—is much more difficult. The best way is to keep detailed records of your speed and direction throughout the voyage. You can use this along with your last known position to get a good idea of where you are now.

Using an astrolabe

North Star

Measure your speed using a log line. This is a rope with equally spaced knots tied in it, and a weight at the end. Throw the line from the stern. Use an hourglass to time one minute. Count the number of knots that reel out in that time. Multiply that number by 60 to find the ship's speed in knots per hour.

Winding out the log line

Counting the knots

Timing using an hourglass

Lead

Log line

Weights attached to log line

Examining the lead for mud or sand stuck to the tallow

Tallow

Lead weight

You need to know how deep the water is close to shore so that you don't run aground. To find out the water's depth, drop a lead weight on a marked line overboard. Sticky tallow (animal fat) on the base of the lead weight will pick up mud from the sea bed. The type of mud can tell a skilled navigator how close the ship is to shore.

Sailing the Ship

You will have to sail your ship in all kinds of weather and sea conditions using only the power of the wind. The master, boatswain, and helm must be skilled in adjusting the sails to steer the ship safely through dangerous seas. The ship has three masts, each with one or two sails. The fore mast and main mast have two square sails. The mizzen mast has a triangular lateen sail.

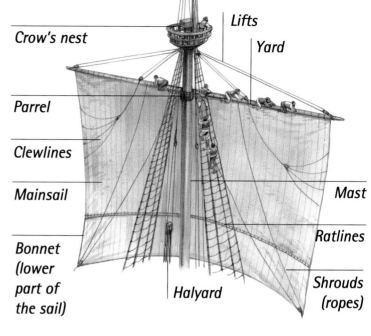

Crow's nest
Lifts
Yard
Parrel
Clewlines
Mainsail
Mast
Ratlines
Bonnet (lower part of the sail)
Halyard
Shrouds (ropes)

Sails and the ropes used to control them are called the rigging. A sail is attached to the mast on a horizontal yard, held in place by lifts. It is hoisted into position by the halyards (ropes used to pull up sails, flags, or yards). Clewlines furl (wrap) the sail up on the yard. The crew climb up the rigging on rope ladders, or ratlines.

Lateen sail is furled

Wind direction

Topsail

Topsail

Mainsail

STERN

Foresail

BOW

To travel in the same direction as the wind, brace the sails at right angles to the wind.

Sprit sail

To change direction, adjust the angle of the square sails and unfurl the lateen sail to catch the wind. The ship will swing around.

You must adjust the position of the sails to change direction in a constant wind, or to keep to your course if the wind changes direction. The yards that support the sails are mounted on the masts using a swivel device, called a parrel. This lets the yards, and therefore the sails, be moved around very easily.

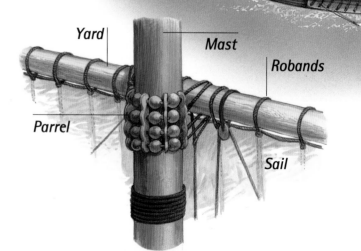

Yard
Mast
Robands
Parrel
Sail

Helm   Pilot

Whipstaff

The helm steers the ship using a long handle, called a whipstaff. This is attached to the rudder at the back of the ship through a series of linked wooden rods. The helm stands on a platform below deck. He can see the sails through a hole in the ceiling. The pilot tells the helm which way to move the whipstaff.

Wind in the ship's sails gives it the power to move forward. Move the sails and rudder to steer the ship. To move the rudder, the helm pushes the whipstaff in the opposite direction from the way the ship should move. To slow down, the crew reduces the amount of sail facing into the wind. This can be done by turning the sails parallel to the wind, or by furling (wrapping up) the sails.

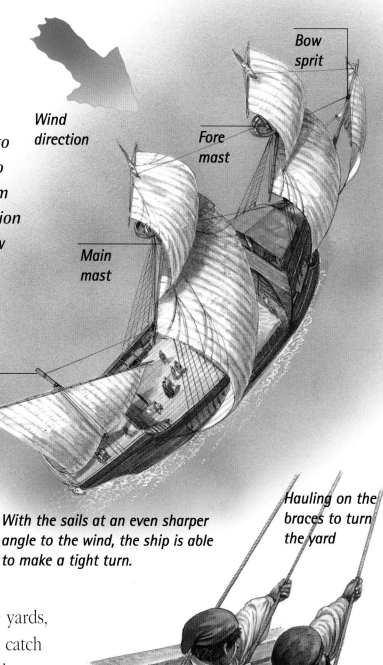

Bow sprit

Wind direction

Fore mast

Main mast

Mizzen mast

With the sails at an even sharper angle to the wind, the ship is able to make a tight turn.

Hauling on the braces to turn the yard

Braces, ropes attached to the ends of the yards, are used to swing the yards around. To catch the wind, brace the yards at right angles to the wind's direction so that the sails fill up.

If you don't need the power of the wind because you want to slow down or keep your position, brace the sails parallel to the wind direction instead.

Mutineers and Privateers

It is very important that you keep order on the ship with so many people on board. Punish any crew members who do not follow orders swiftly and fairly. Work closely with the captain of the soldiers to make sure the troops are kept under strict control. Watch out for dangers outside the ship, too. Attacks from pirates and privateers are a constant danger.

Ship's officer listening in

Plotting mutineers

Sailors often complain about their harsh life. But if they start to talk about mutiny, where they would take control of the ship from the captain and officers, you should act at once.

Mutineers in chains

Ship's master

Troublemakers should be arrested at the first sign of unrest. Have your master lock them in the hold away from the rest of the crew. Down there they can't encourage others to rebel. You might decide to punish them quickly and let them return to their duties after they've calmed down. Or you might have them officially charged with a crime once you reach port.

Crow's nest

Keep a look out for enemy ships at all times. Your crew must tell you at once if they spot a suspicious vessel.

Enemy ship

Your ship firing at the enemy's bow

Raking is one way to attack an enemy that you can't outrun. But use it only if you think you can out-fire them.

You have three choices when faced with an attack. You can flee, but a fast pirate ship would almost certainly catch up. You can surrender and hope your enemy will spare your ship and your lives. This is often the best choice against a strong enemy. The last option is to fight.

To launch a counterattack, get your gunners into position. Order your crew to put anti-boarding nets over the deck. If the attackers get close enough to board, they will get tangled in these. You'll then have a chance to overpower them.

Position your ship's side directly in front of the pirate ship's bow. Fire your cannon straight down the pirate ship's length. This is called raking. If you hit your target, you can shatter the hull from bow to stern.

Putting up anti-boarding nets

Enemy mast smashed by cannon fire

21

Storms and Shipwrecks

Storms and bad weather are a risk on any voyage. The seas around the southern coast of Africa are very rough. Try to schedule your trip for when storms are less likely. Be prepared in case the worst occurs. Make sure your crew are ready to man the sails quickly if necessary. Your lookout should warn you right away if it looks like bad weather is approaching.

Mainsail partially furled

Boatswain instructing the crew to furl the sails

Topsail

Crow's nest

Foresail

Boatswain

At the first sign of bad weather, instruct your boatswain to trim the sails. You need to furl most of the sails in, so that the ship is not flung in all directions by the wind, and the sails are not ripped apart by the gales. However, you need to leave some sail up, so that you still have control. If you have no sail at all, your ship will be tossed like a empty box on the sea.

Bowsprit sail ripped by storm

There are several things you can do to prevent a shipwreck in a bad storm. Put out any stoves or candles on board to make sure fire does not break out. Keep the bilges pumped out around the clock to get rid of any water coming into the ship.

If the ship is close to sinking, order passengers and crew to throw any unnecessary weight overboard as a last resort. You might have to throw cannons, ammunition, food stores, and even precious cargo overboard.

Sinking ship

Launch

If you have to abandon ship, use the launch to get as many people off the vessel as possible. If you are close to shore, the launch can make several trips between ship and land. Collect as much food and supplies as you can from the wreckage. These things might also wash up on shore. But don't stay on the beach, where it may not be safe. Have your people march inland to look for a camp or settlement.

Silks and Spices

Congratulations! You have arrived safely in the busy port of Goa. If you are on schedule, you will have several weeks to load up your ship and get ready for the voyage home.

Make sure any repairs to your ship are done right away. Some of your crew might have died from diseases or injuries on the outbound voyage. Tell your master to hire extra crew members to take their place.

The master should also restock the ship's food and water supplies. Trade any goods you have brought from Europe. Arrange for pepper and other official cargo to be delivered to your ship.

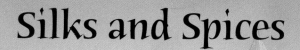

Buying silk

You must make sure that the pepper for the king is of good quality. Check the weight and quality with the Indian merchants and with the factor. The factor is the king's official representative here. The pepper must not be damp or dirty. Once you've checked that it's okay, have it loaded on to your ship. Your crewmen can buy spices, silks, and china in the busy markets to take home and sell.

Factor's clerk

Do not overload your ship with supplies and luxury goods you and your passengers have bought in Goa. An overloaded ship is unstable. It could sink in rough seas around the Cape of Good Hope. Passengers might try to bribe you to let them have more cargo space. Resist this temptation. Load your ship carefully, and set sail for home no later than December.

Recruiting

Fleet

Indian merchant

Factor

Weighing peppercorns

Checking the quality of the peppercorns

Timeline

In the 15th century, Portugal was the first European country to send out voyages to explore the world beyond Europe. Portugal made very successful expeditions to North and West Africa. One main reason for this was the support of the Portuguese Prince Henry, known as the Navigator.

Vasco da Gama

The Silk Road was the overland trade route running between Asia and Europe. When it was closed by Muslim rulers in the mid-1400s, Portugal set out to find a sea route to the East around the tip of Africa instead.

In 1487, Bartholomeu Dias was the first European to sail around the Cape of Good Hope. Ten years later, Vasco da Gama discovered a route around Africa and across the Indian Ocean to India. Portugal set up colonies in India as soon as possible.

From those settlements, the Portuguese opened up trade with Southeast Asia, China, and Japan. Trading spices especially brought great wealth and power to Portugal, who controlled the sea route from Lisbon to India for most of the 16th century.

1394
Henry the Navigator, son of King Juan I of Portugal, is born.

1415
Portugal occupies Ceuta (Spanish Morocco) on the north coast of Africa, an important center of the spice trade.

1419
Portuguese explorers Zarco and Tristão Vaz Teixeira explore the Madeira Islands off the west coast of Africa.

1432
Portuguese navigator Diogo Silves lands on the Azores in the North Atlantic.

1434
Portuguese exploration of the west coast of Africa begins.

1450
Prince Henry the Navigator establishes a naval school for teaching navigation, map reading, and cartography (map-making).

1453
The Turks overrun Constantinople, shutting off the overland trade routes from Asia to Europe.

1487
Bartholomeu Dias leads a Portuguese expedition around the Cape of Good Hope.

1492
Christopher Columbus, sailing on behalf of Spain, arrives in the Western Hemisphere, which Europeans called the New World.

Columbus's ships sail across the Atlantic Ocean

On board Magellan's ship

1494

Spain and Portugal sign the Treaty of Tordesillas. This treaty divides South America between the two countries. Portugal gains control over Brazil, while Spain gains control over the rest of South America.

1497–8

Vasco da Gama rounds the Cape of Good Hope and reaches India, opening up a major trade route to the East.

1500

Portuguese explorer Pedro Alvares Cabral arrives in Brazil.

1502

Amerigo Vespucci, an Italian who sails on behalf of Portugal, returns from the so-called New World. The Americas are named after him.

1510

Alfonso de Albuquerque takes control of Goa for Portugal.

1511

Portugal takes control of the Spice Islands (Maluku) in Indonesia.

1519

Ferdinand Magellan leads the first voyage around the world for Spain.

1521

Hernán Cortés defeats the Aztec Empire in Mexico for Spain.

1530

Portugal sets up colonies in Brazil.

1533

Francisco Pizarro defeats the Inca Empire in South America for Spain.

1542

Portuguese sailors are the first Europeans to land in Japan.

1580

Philip II of Spain defeats Portugal at the Battle of Alcantara near Lisbon. This battle unites Spain and Portugal, but Portugal keeps some independence. Trade with India continues as before.

1599

Holland establishes the first Dutch trading posts in the Spice Islands.

1600s

Holland gradually gains control of the spice trade from Portugal.

Glossary

aft Toward the rear of the ship, or the stern.

astrolabe A navigational instrument that measures the height of the sun and stars and helps with finding latitude.

ballast Any heavy material, such as stones, placed low in a vessel to increase stability.

bilges The lowest part of a ship where any water in the hull collects. The bilges need to be pumped free of water from time to time.

bow The forward part of a ship's hull.

carrack Large, square-rigged ship with two to four masts. Called a nau in Portugal.

compass A magnetic device that always points north. Used in navigation.

cross-staff An instrument for measuring the altitude of the sun or stars. It consists of a shaft and a sliding cross-piece.

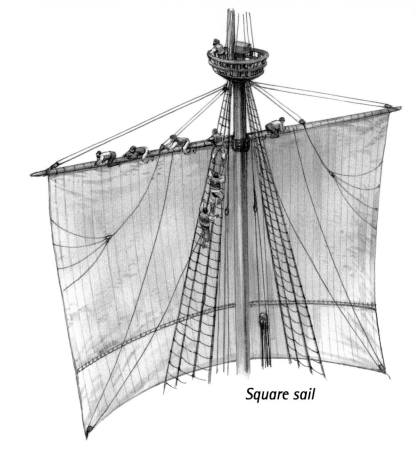

Square sail

Equator An imaginary circle around the Earth, halfway between the two poles.

fore Toward the front of a ship, or the bow.

hourglass A device for measuring time (not always a full hour). Two glass globes are connected by a narrow neck. Sand empties from the top globe into the bottom one within a certain amount of time.

lateen A triangular sail set at an angle to a short mast.

latitude The distance north or south of the Equator. The Equator has a latitude of zero degrees. The North Pole has a latitude of 90 degrees north; the South Pole has a latitude of 90 degrees south.

A band of privateers

lead line A rope with length markings attached to a lead weight. Used to measure depth.

log line and reel A device for measuring a ship's speed. A weight is attached to a rope with equally spaced knots tied in it. The weight is then dropped into the water. The number of knots that reel out within a certain amount of time give the ship's speed.

Hourglass

longitude The distance east or west from a north-south line that passes through Greenwich, England. Greenwich has a longitude of zero degrees.

mast A vertical pole, usually made of wood, that supports yards and sails.

monsoon Strong seasonal winds that bring heavy rainfall to a region.

navigation Plotting or directing the course of a ship using instruments such as a compass.

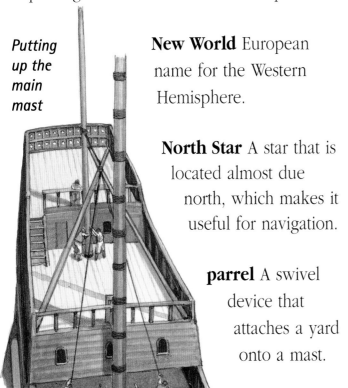

Putting up the main mast

New World European name for the Western Hemisphere.

North Star A star that is located almost due north, which makes it useful for navigation.

parrel A swivel device that attaches a yard onto a mast.

pilot A person who navigates a vessel.

privateer A ship and crew hired by a government to attack an enemy country's ships.

rudder A device mounted near the stern of a vessel that controls the ship's direction.

scurvy A disease caused by a lack of vitamin C, which is found mainly in fresh fruit and vegetables.

Silk Road Overland trading routes between Asia and Europe.

stern The rear or aft part of the ship's hull.

trade winds Strong winds that blow from the northeast in the Northern Hemisphere and from the southeast in the Southern Hemisphere. Helped trade ships reach their destinations in the Western Hemisphere.

whipstaff A vertical pole linked to the rudder.

yard The pole on a mast that carries a sail.

Further Reading

Books

Bailey, Katharine. *Vasco de Gama: Quest for the Spice Trade*. New York: Crabtree Publishing, 2007.

Rodger, Ellen. *The Biography of Spices*. New York: Crabtree Publishing, 2006.

Wells, Donald. *The Spice Trade*. New York: Weigl Publishers, 2005.

Internet Addresses

EXPLORERS
http://www.enchantedlearning.com/explorers/1500a.shtml

THE HISTORY OF THE SPICE TRADE IN INDIA
http://www.english.emory.edu/Bahri/Spice_Trade.html

NAVIGATION METHODS
http://www.heritage.nf.ca/exploration/navigate.html

Index